THIS BOOK BELONGS TO

Written by James Clements and Jo Nelson
With additional material by Tom Evans

PUFFIN BOOKS

UK | USA | Canada | Ireland | Australia
India | New Zealand | South Africa

Puffin Books is part of the Penguin Random House group of companies
whose addresses can be found at global.penguinrandomhouse.com.
www.penguin.co.uk    www.puffin.co.uk    www.ladybird.co.uk

Roald Dahl quotations from *James and the Giant Peach* (1961, 2022), *Charlie and the Chocolate Factory* (1964, 2022), *Fantastic Mr Fox* (1970, 2022), *Rhyme Stew* (1989, 2017), *Matilda* (1988, 2023), *The BFG* (1982, 2022), *The Giraffe and the Pelly and Me* (1985, 2022), *The Witches* (1983, 2022), *George's Marvellous Medicine* (1981, 2022), *Charlie and the Great Glass Elevator* (1972, 2022) and *James and the Giant Peach: The Play* (1982, 2017). All titles are published by Puffin Books or Penguin Books.
Selected material from *Roald Dahl Creative Writing with James and the Giant Peach: How to Write Phenomenal Poetry* (2020), *Roald Dahl Creative Writing with The BFG: How to Write Splendid Settings* (2019) and *Roald Dahl Creative Writing with Matilda: How to Write Spellbinding Speech* (2019), all published by Puffin Books.
First published 2025
001

Printed in China

The authorized representative in the EEA is Penguin Random House Ireland,
Morrison Chambers, 32 Nassau Street, Dublin D02 YH68

A CIP catalogue record for this book is available from the British Library

ISBN: 978–0–241–61078–7

All correspondence to:
Puffin Books
Penguin Random House Children's
One Embassy Gardens, 8 Viaduct Gardens, London SW11 7BW

# ROALD DAHL

# How to Be a Writer

## GLORIUMPTIOUS POETRY

# CONTENTS

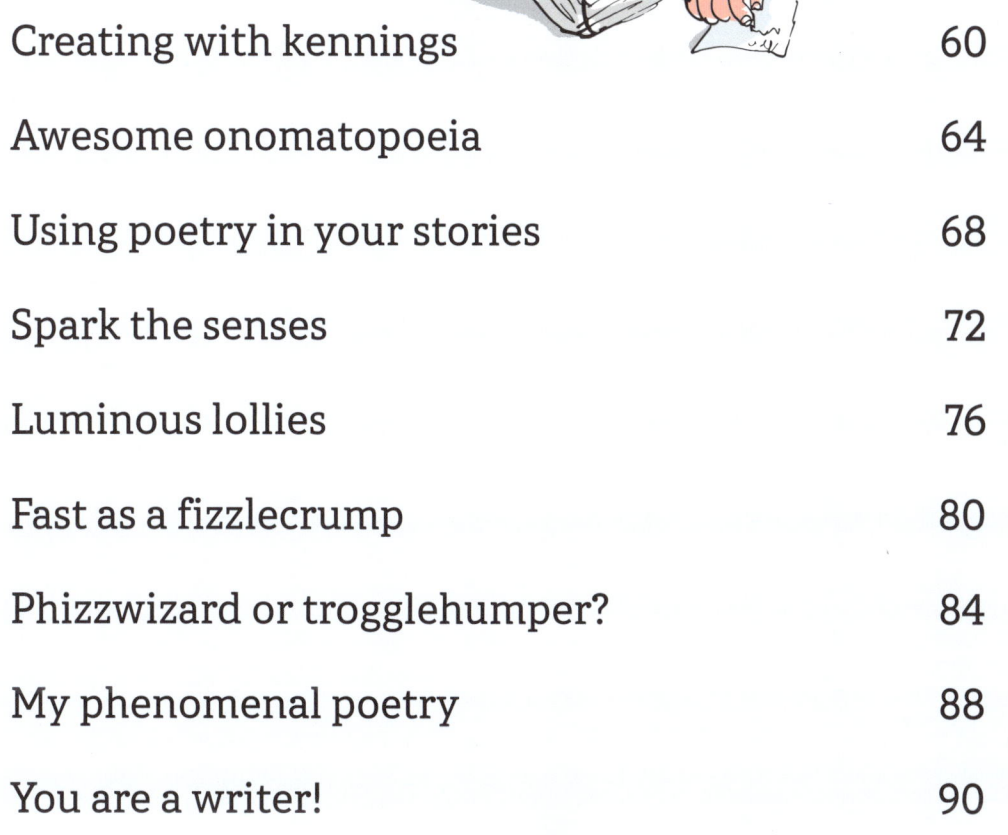

# HOW TO USE THIS BOOK

Get ready! You are about to become an amazing poet! Poetry can be used everywhere, and poems come in all shapes and sizes – they can be funny or serious, rhyming or not, and can look however you want them to. You will learn about different types of poems, but you can break the rules or make up your own type of poem whenever you like. Anyone can be a poet, so start writing and have fun!

Make sure you have the following things before you start: pens, pencils and an eraser. If you have a dictionary and a thesaurus, they will come in handy, too.

As you go through this book, look out for lots of tips, tricks and fun ideas that will help you along the way.

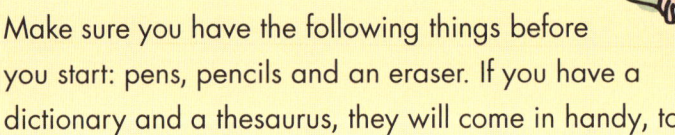

When you are writing poetry, think carefully about the language you use. You can spend lots of time choosing the right word to share an idea.

If you choose to write a rhyming poem, it can be helpful to jot down some rhyming words first. You can also use a rhyming dictionary to help you.

Arrange the words carefully so they carry the meaning, rhythm and sound that you want to share.

Think about how you want your reader to feel. Do you want them to laugh? To understand something new? This will affect the words you choose and the particular rhythm of your poem.

Whether your poem is rhyming or not, it is always important to think about the rhythm of the words.

You might use similes and metaphors in your poem to share an idea in a beautiful, funny or believable way.

Poems don't just have to appear in books. Many poems are written to be performed out loud. You can plan which parts will be loud, quiet, fast and slow.

You can use the language of poetry in all your writing. Try using a simile or a metaphor in a story, or include a funny rhyme in a friend's birthday card.

# POETRY AND RHYTHM

Poetry is a special type of writing. There are many different types and styles of poems. Some are simple, and some are complicated. Some are funny, while others are very serious.

Lots of poems have a particular rhythm. The rhythm of a poem depends on how many syllables or "beats" each line has. The word "writer" has two syllables: wri-ter, and the word "poetry" has three: po-e-try.

Read the Centipede's poem from *James and the Giant Peach* out loud, and clap along.

*I've eaten many strange and scrumptious dishes in my time,*

*Like jellied gnats and dandyprats and earwigs cooked in slime,*

*And mice with rice – they're really nice*

*When roasted in their prime.*

*(But don't forget to sprinkle them with just a pinch of grime.)*

- Which word in the poem has the most syllables? _____

- And which words have the fewest syllables? _____

_____

_____

- Can you think of some other words that have the same number of syllables as "sprinkle"?

_____

8

Here are some of the other foods the Centipede loves to eat. Clap along and count the number of syllables in each one.

hot-frogs [ ]        hot noodles made from poodles [ ]

crispy wasp-stings [ ]        tasty tentacles of octopi [ ]

smelly jelly [ ]        curried slugs [ ]        scrambled dregs [ ]

Now read the Centipede's poem out loud again, and count the syllables in each line. Write the number of syllables below.

| | |
|---|---|
| *I've eaten many strange and scrumptious dishes in my time,* | 14 |
| *Like jellied gnats and dandyprats and earwigs cooked in slime,* | |
| *And mice with rice – they're really nice* | |
| *When roasted in their prime.* | |
| *(But don't forget to sprinkle them with just a pinch of grime.)* | |

In this poem, Roald Dahl has thought carefully about the rhythm. Can you spot a pattern in the number of syllables he has used? What is it?

_____

_____

Now invent some more disgusting foods for the Centipede. Write them down, then count the syllables in each one.

poached leg of toad        4

Can't think of an idea? Ask other people! Ask your grown-ups, brothers, sisters or friends. Definitely ask your grown-ups about the sort of food they used to hate when they were your age!

Can you use your disgusting food to finish the 'Centipede's Shopping List' poem below?
Count the syllables in each line to try to give your poem a regular rhythm.

## Centipede's Shopping List

Gorilla's toes and catfish nose,

Rotten turnip, eggs and jam,

# RADIANT RHYMES

Words rhyme when they sound similar - usually because they share the same vowel sound. (Vowels are the letters a, e, i, o and u.) Poems don't have to rhyme, but a lot of them do!

Can you think of words that rhyme? They may be in your favourite book or song, or you could even look at the things around you. Write some rhyming words below.

nose/toes

trap/snap

**Did you know?**

There are some words in English that don't rhyme with anything! They include: orange, month, silver, purple, dangerous, wolf and marathon.

In *Charlie and the Chocolate Factory*, the Oompa-Loompas sing this poem about Augustus Gloop. Use different colours to underline the words that rhyme.

Augustus Gloop! Augustus Gloop!

The great big greedy nincompoop!

For one such child as vile as he

Bad things happen, wait and see!

We cannot say we are surprised,

Augustus Gloop had been advised.

The poem below is from *Fantastic Mr Fox*. This type of poem is called a limerick. Can you see a rhyming pattern in the poem?

Limericks always have five lines and are often funny. The first, second and fifth lines are longer and always rhyme. The third and fourth lines are shorter, and they rhyme, too.

Boggis and Bunce and Bean

One fat, one short, one lean.

These horrible crooks

So different in looks

Were none the less equally mean.

Plan a limerick of your own in the space below. You could write about someone you know, a creature or character from one of Roald Dahl's books, or a new character entirely. Think of some rhyming words that might help you.

If you can't find a word that rhymes perfectly, you can use half-rhymes. These are words that share some, but not all, of the same sounds. For example, "wavy" and "baby", or "market" and "carpet".

Now write your limerick!

## Rhyming challenge

You can learn lots of rhyming words by
playing rhyming games. Ask a friend to
give you a word, then you have to think
of as many words as possible that
rhyme with it. Write them all down!

# TELLING A STORY

Poems that tell a story are called narrative poems. Narrative poems do not need to rhyme, but they usually have a clear rhythm.

Read the extract from Roald Dahl's narrative poem below. Think of different words that could go in the gaps, and make notes in the shapes on the opposite page. Then fill in the gaps in the poem.

## The Dentist and the Crocodile

The crocodile, with cunning smile, sat in the dentist's _____.

He said, "Right here and everywhere my teeth require repair."

The dentist's _____ was turning white. He quivered, quaked and _____.

He muttered, "I suppose I'm going to have to take a look."

"I want you," Crocodile declared, "to do the back ones first.

The molars at the very back are easily the _____."

He opened wide his massive jaws. It was a fearsome sight —

At least three hundred pointed _____, all sharp and shining _____.

The dentist kept himself well clear. He stood two yards away.

He chose the longest probe he had to search out the _____.

"I said to do the *back ones* first!" the Crocodile called _____.

"You're much too far _____, dear sir, to see what you're about.

To do the back ones properly you've got to put your head

Deep down inside my great big _____," the grinning Crocky _____.

The poor old dentist wrung his hands and, weeping in despair,

He cried, "No no! I see them all extremely well from _____!"

house

hair

Can you write a narrative poem of your own?
Answer the questions below to plan your poem.
Use the ideas box for extra help.

What is your poem about?

What happens?

Note down any useful words or phrases you might include in your poem.
Can you think of any pairs of rhyming words?

Many narrative poems are written in couplets. This is when every two lines rhyme and have the same rhythm. Why not give it a go?

Now write your poem. Remember, it doesn't have to rhyme, but try to keep to a regular rhythm (see page 8).

# ASTOUNDING ACROSTICS

In an acrostic poem, the first letter of each line spells out a word or phrase. This gives you a clear structure for your poem. Acrostic poems do not have to rhyme or even keep a regular rhythm.

**S**pinning silk so long and strong,

**P**erfect legs – eight of those,

**I**nside burrows or on webs,

**D**ining on what she can catch,

**E**very shadow and corner,

**R**adiant webs glisten in the light.

Read the example above. Plan your own animal acrostic poem in the boxes below.

Animal:

A picture of your animal

Useful words and phrases

Now write your acrostic poem.

## Acrostic names

A good way to practise acrostic poems is to write one using your name. Think about all the things you know about yourself. Use those facts to fill in each line.

Now think about a person you know. It could be a friend or family member, a character from a story or a famous person. Plan an acrostic poem about them in the boxes below. Can you use some of the ideas you've learned about in this book?

Person:

A picture of the person

Useful words and phrases

Now write your acrostic poem.

## Acrostic challenge!

Write a double acrostic poem! This means that the last letter of each line has to be the same as the first letter. This way, you write your acrostic word twice!

# HEY THERE, HAIKU

A haiku is a type of poem that was first written in Japan. Haiku always have three lines. The first line has five syllables, the second line has seven syllables and the final line has five syllables.

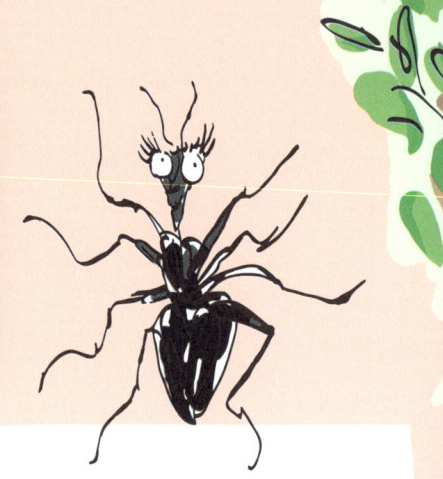

Match each haiku to the correct character below.

Amazing creature,
• • •   • • (5)
A lamp shining in the dark.
• •   • •   • • (7)
Her tail is glowing.
• •   • • • (5)

What a lot of shoes –
•   • •   • •
And so many feet for them.
• •   • •   • •
Help him put them on!
•   •   •   •

Gliding underground,
• •   • •   • •
A friend of the gardener.
• •   • •   • •
Cannot see too far.
• •   • •   •

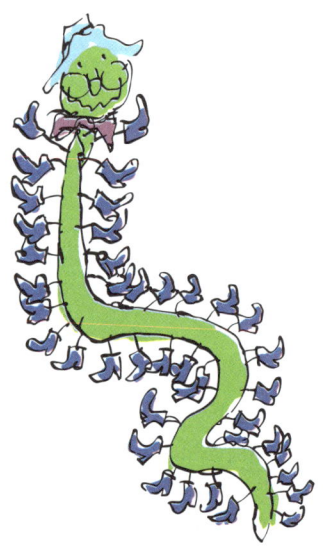

Think of a place you know well. Make some notes about this place.

What is its name?

Where is it?

How does it smell?

What does it look like?

What words could you use to describe your place?
How many syllables does each word have?

Haiku can be tricky to write because they are so short, but they help you to think carefully about the words you use. Only use the most important, striking words!

**One syllable**

home

**Two syllables**

visit

**Three syllables**

favourite

**Four or more syllables**

environment

Now write two haiku about the place you have chosen. Try to make each one different. Once you've written each haiku, read it through and edit it to make it as good as it can be!

**1**

**2**

Show your haiku to someone who knows the place you've written about. Can they guess where it is?

# PERFORMING POEMS

Poems don't have to stay on the page. Many poems are written to be performed or read aloud!

Read the poem below from *Charlie and the Chocolate Factory*. How would you perform it? Use one colour to underline the parts you would read loudly. Use another colour to underline the parts you would read quietly.

*There's no earthly way of knowing*

*Which direction they are going!*

*There's no knowing where they're rowing,*

*Or which way the river's flowing!*

*Not a speck of light is showing,*

*So the danger must be growing,*

*For the rowers keep on rowing,*

*And they're certainly not showing*

*Any signs that they are slowing . . .*

Read the poem again. Would some bits be quick, slow, whispered or shouted? Could you do any actions as you are reading? Plan your performance in the space below. You can make notes around the poem, too.

Rehearse the poem a few times to get your performance right before you show it to someone else!

Now read the poem aloud. Is there anything you would change about your performance?

## Putting on a show

What else can you add to your performance? Are there any actions you can do while performing? What sound effects could you make?

Choose one poem you have written in this book so far. Write the poem out in the space below. Add some notes to help you perform it. If you want to edit your poem as you write it out, then you can!

## Practice makes perfect

Have a go at reading your poem in lots of different ways.
Can you perform your poem:

- as quietly as you can?
- as slowly as you can?
- while brushing your teeth?
- while standing on one leg?

Perform the poem for someone else. What did they think? Record their thoughts below.

They really liked:

_____

_____

_____

_____

Next time, I could:

_____

_____

_____

_____

Now you've performed your poem, what advice would you give to others? Write your own top tips for performing poetry below.

# WONDERFUL WORDS

No matter what type of poem you write, it is important to think carefully about the words you use. Choosing the right words can make your poem sound wonderful.

Read the story text from *Matilda* below, where Miss Trunchbull and Miss Honey are first introduced. Underline the adjectives (or describing words) that are used.

*Miss Jennifer Honey was a mild and quiet person who never raised her voice and was seldom seen to smile, but there is no doubt she possessed that rare gift for being adored by every small child under her care . . .*

*Miss Trunchbull, the Headmistress, was something else altogether. She was a gigantic holy terror, a fierce tyrannical monster who frightened the life out of the pupils and teachers alike.*

## The right words

Interesting adjectives make interesting poems! You could describe someone as "nice", but it's not as exciting as saying they're "amazing". Think of some enthralling alternatives for these words:

| big | scary | little | hard | hot |
|-----|-------|--------|------|-----|

Now look at Miss Trunchbull and Miss Honey. What adjectives would you use to describe them? Write them in the space below.

fierce

friendly

**Miss Trunchbull**

**Miss Honey**

The right verb (or doing word) can help the reader to picture the ideas in your poem more clearly, too. Think of different verbs to describe how Miss Trunchbull and Miss Honey might behave.

| | **Miss Trunchbull** | **Miss Honey** |
|---|---|---|
| **running** | galloping | |
| **speaking** | | |
| **dancing** | | |
| **closing** a door | | |
| **walking** | | |

A thesaurus isn't a type of dinosaur. It's like a dictionary, but instead of telling you what a word means it suggests other words that mean the same thing – like "jump" and "leap".

Use your adjectives and verbs to write a poem about Miss Trunchbull and Miss Honey. You will need an adjective for each short line and a verb for each long line. Remember, it doesn't have to rhyme!

## Trunchbull and Honey

Miss Trunchbull was ___breathless___ as she ___thundered along the road___ .

Miss Honey was _____ as she _____ .

Miss Trunchbull was _____ as she _____ .

Miss Honey was _____ as she _____ .

Miss Trunchbull was _____ as she _____ .

Miss Honey was _____ as she _____ .

Read your poem again. Can you make any changes so the rhythm is the same in each line? Turn back to page 8 for more information on rhythm!

Writing poetry can help you to think differently about the words you use in your stories, too.

# SWASHBOGGLING SYNONYMS

There are lots of different descriptive words. When a word has the same meaning as another word, it is called a synonym.

The things in Mr Fox's world seem very small to humans. Think of some synonyms for the adjective "small", and write them in this space.

tiny

**small**

Now write down all the synonyms you can think of for the adjective "dark".

murky

**dark**

Use the synonyms from the opposite page to write a descriptive poem about
Mr Fox's underground home.

Everything where you live is much bigger than the things in Mr Fox's home! How many synonyms do you know for the adjective "big"?

huge

**big**

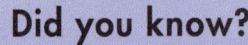

### Did you know?

The opposite of a synonym is an antonym. For example, the antonym of "hot" is "cold". Can you think of some antonyms of the words you have written on this page?

Write a poem about where you live from Mr Fox's point of view.
Try to use different synonyms for the adjective "big".

There are lots of ways to describe the same place. Writers often use different adjectives to introduce the same setting!

# FLUSHBUNKING AND GLORIUMPTIOUS

Roald Dahl's stories use very inventive and playful words. You can join two descriptive words with a hyphen to make a completely new word, like "twitch-tickling"!

Draw lines between the jars to make your own hyphenated words for your poetry.

| | |
|---|---|
| noisy- | fizzy |
| butter- | gobbling |
| munch- | booky |
| jumpy- | cracking |
| dream- | hopping |

*"What a phizz-whizzing flushbunking seat!"*

*"What a spliffling whoppsy room we is in!"*

What is your favourite new word from the jars?

What could it mean?

You can also invent words by taking a word you already know, then adding a new suffix (or ending) to it. Use the ideas box to write some brand-new words below. This time, you don't need the hyphens.

The BFG says lots of words that you wouldn't find in a dictionary, but you can still understand what he means!

## Ideas box

| Words | Suffixes |
|-------|----------|
| luck | -able |
| dark | -some |
| gloom | -ing |
| joy | -wise |
| silver | -ful |
| dirt | -ness |
| wonder | -ous |

You can even mix words up! The adjectives "glorious", "scrumptious" and "delicious" can be mixed together to make *gloriumptious*, *delumptious* and *glumptious*.

Mix up these words to make some new adjectives for your poetry.

disgusting + repulsive + horrible

cheerful + happy + delighted

foul + revolting + pongy

beautiful + charming + superb

Use some of your favourite new words in a sentence.

Now try inventing some brand-new synonyms (words that mean the same thing as each other) for the adjectives below. You can use any of the ideas on this page or think of some of your own.

**excellent**

squiffling

**light**

wispy-misty

**wet**

quelchy

**cold**

frisby

## Letter jumble!

Make your own wonderful words! Write letters on pieces of paper, and put them into a box. Then take out random letters to create fun new words!

# BRILLIANT ADVERBS

You can make your poems more expressive by using adverbs. Adverbs describe verbs, adjectives or other adverbs. These words tell us how, when, where, how often or how much.

Here are some adverbs to describe how characters might speak or act in your poem. Write the opposite of each adverb on the lines.

kindly

fearfully

wisely

boldly

deceitfully

She spoke _quietly_ and _politely_ and without any sign of showing off.

Adverbs often end in -ly.

What other adverbs can you think of to show how someone speaks? Write as many as you can in the space below.

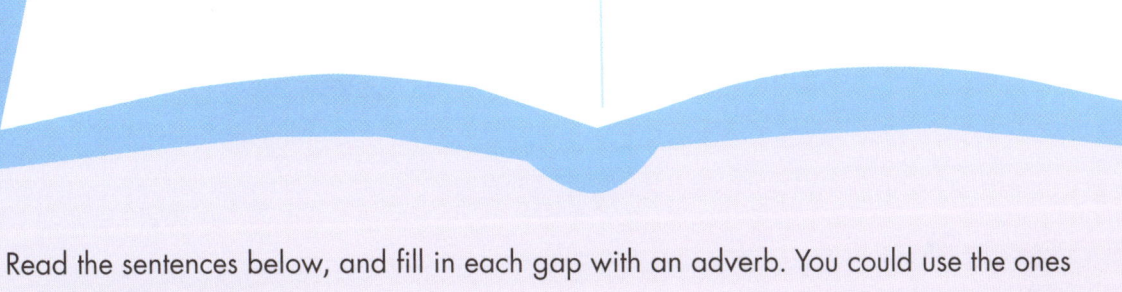

Read the sentences below, and fill in each gap with an adverb. You could use the ones you thought of earlier.

"And to think I invented that all by myself," he added _____.

"I don't quite know," Matilda said _____.

"I am trying to explain to you," Miss Honey said _____, "that we are dealing with the unknown."

"I don't want to go with them!" Matilda shouted _____.

Look at the picture, and read the story text.
What adverbs could you use to describe the
way Matilda is speaking? Write them below.

*She trotted beside
Miss Honey with wild
little hops and her fingers
flew as if she would
scatter them to the four
winds and her words
went off like fireworks,
with terrific speed.*

excitedly

Think of a character who likes to show off. What adverbs
could you use in a poem to describe them?

loudly

Write a poem about your friend telling you something incredible! Use interesting adverbs with "said", and remember to use the correct punctuation.

There are lots of adverbs that don't end with the suffix -ly. For example, "best" and "today".

# AMAZING ALLITERATION

Alliteration is where words start with the same sound. You can use alliteration to make your readers focus on particular words in your poem, or to create different effects.

Look at these characters and objects. Can you think of some alliterative adjectives for each one?

**Peach**

perfect

**Shark**

shiny

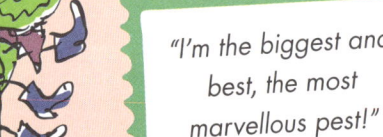

"I'm the biggest and best, the most marvellous pest!"

## Glow-worm

gleeful

"A Gnu and a Gnocerous
surely you'll see
And that gnormous and
gnorrible Gnat"

## James

gentle

Use your adjectives to write some alliterative phrases below.

The perfectly plump peach

Characters' names can be alliterative, too. Can you think of an alliterative name for each character below?

Willy Wonka

Boggis, Bunce and Bean

Bruce Bogtrotter

A strong warrior _____

A great ballet dancer _____

A very clever burglar _____

An evil genius _____

When you use lots of alliterative words, you can end up with a tongue-twister! Try saying this one really fast.

**The Old-Green-Grasshopper gathered garish, golden garments.**

Write some tongue-twisters about the characters below.

Miss Spider spied _____

_____

The lovely Ladybird _____

_____ .

You can also choose to use more than one word with the same vowel sound. This is called assonance. Try writing a poem with repeated vowel sounds. Use the ideas box for extra help.

Freezes and sneezes and noses will blow!

## Ideas box

| moon | high | queen |
|------|------|-------|
| blue | my | seed |
| blew | fire | dream |
| broom | delight | uneasy |
| soup | wide | hungry |
| grew | dive | been |
| stew | wise | marry |

# SUPER SIMILES

When you compare things using "as" or "like", it is called a simile!
Similes help the reader to picture something in your poem.
They can also help you to use words more creatively.

Read this poem from *The Giraffe and the Pelly and Me.*

*We will polish your glass*

*Till it's shining <u>like</u> brass*

*And it sparkles <u>like</u> sun on the sea!*

*We are quick and polite,*

*We will come day or night,*

*The Giraffe and the Pelly and me!*

Draw a picture of someone you know. Think of similes to describe them, then write them down.

**My drawing**

Look at the Giraffe, the Pelly, the Monkey, the Duke and Billy. Finish the similes below to describe them.

The Giraffe's neck is as long as _____

_____ .

The Monkey's tail is like _____

_____ .

The Pelly's beak is as big as _____

_____ .

Billy's T-shirt is red like _____

_____ .

The Duke's trousers are green like _____

_____ .

Write a simile to describe each character from *The Giraffe and the Pelly and Me*.

**Monkey**

**Pelly**

**Giraffe**

**The Duke**

Now think of an animal. It might be a character from a story, an animal you know or one you have made up. Write a simile poem to describe the animal.

_____ is as _____ as a _____

_____

_____

_____

_____

_____

## Simile starters

We're going to work backwards! Can you think of sentences that end with these similes?

_____

_____ like a bit of mouldy banana.

_____

_____ as though the stars shone inside.

# MAGNIFICENT METAPHORS

Poets sometimes make comparisons without using "as" or "like". These comparisons are called metaphors. They help to share an idea and tell the reader something special.

Often a metaphor isn't true, but it can help the reader to understand a character or situation the poet is describing.

> *My blood turned to ice.*

Read the metaphors below. Draw lines to join each metaphor to the character it describes best.

A brilliant scientist

He was a giant with tree trunks for legs and arms carved from granite.

A champion athlete

Her brain was a computer.

A wrestler

He was a little porcupine, covered in prickles.

A grumpy child

She was a cheetah on the running track.

Choose one of the characters on the opposite page. Can you think of some more metaphors to describe them?

**Did you know?**

Similes and metaphors are both examples of figurative language.

## Metaphorical makings

Can you think of metaphors for these things?

- Snow on the ground

- A friend that makes you laugh a lot

- An enormously tall person

A character's name can be a kind of metaphor, too – a clue about what they are like. What do you think these characters' names tell you about them?

Miss Agatha Trunchbull

_____

Miss Jennifer Honey

_____

Mr Harry Wormwood

_____

Imagine another unpleasant head teacher for Matilda. Think of a name that is a metaphor for their behaviour. Use the ideas box for extra help.

**Ideas box**
frightful
moody
wicked
awful

Can you think of a name for a character that:

tells jokes?     _____

is always late?  _____

likes football?  _____

Write a poem about the head teacher you've invented on the opposite page. Use metaphors to describe their character.

Metaphors are perfect in poems, and you can use them when you are writing stories, too. They can help the reader to imagine things very clearly.

# CREATING WITH KENNINGS

Kennings describe a person, place or object by joining words together with a hyphen. Kennings were used long ago by the Vikings in northern Europe.

James might be described with these different kennings.

magic-finder

seagull-catcher

insect-befriender

peach-dweller

Match each kenning to the creature it describes best.

light-giver          web-weaver          boot-wearer          silk-spinner

Think of another kenning to describe each creature.

Miss Spider _____

The Silkworm _____

The Glow-worm _____

The Centipede _____

You can write a whole poem with kennings. The kenning poem could even be a riddle, so the reader has to work out what it is about!

Who or what are these kenning poems about? Write your thoughts in the spaces below.

Night-crier,
Toy-chewer,
Milk-drinker,
Nappy-wearer.

Sea-dweller,
Colour-changer,
Ink-squirter,
Tentacle-waver.

Moonlit-flyer,
Mouse-hunter,
Head-turner,
Hoot-screecher.

What could you write a kenning poem about? Plan your ideas in the spaces below.

Now write your poem.

Similes, metaphors and kennings can all be used to write about something familiar in a new or interesting way.

## Kennings creator

What kenning might you come up with for:

- a teacher?
- a dog?
- a bicycle?
- a kettle?
- a games console?
- a pineapple?

# AWESOME ONOMATOPOEIA

Onomatopoeia describes words that sound like the thing they mean, like "bang", "crash", "crackle" and "hiss". Roald Dahl's stories and poems often use onomatopoeia (or sound words).

There are lots of sound words in *George's Marvellous Medicine*. Read the poem below, then circle all of the examples of onomatopoeia.

*Fiery broth and witch's brew*

*Foamy froth and riches blue*

*Fume and spume and spoondrift spray*

*Fizzle swizzle shout hooray*

*Watch it sloshing, swashing, sploshing*

*Hear it hissing, squishing, spissing*

*Grandma better start to pray.*

### Make some noise!

Have a look for things you can tap, shake or make an interesting sound with. Listen carefully, and have a go at writing onomatopoeic words for the sounds you make!

Can you think of different sound words that might be coming out of George's pan? Write your ideas below.

What things might make these sounds? Write or draw your ideas in the spaces below.

**Pop**

**Hiss**

**Sizzle**

**Splash**

**Drip**

**Crash**

Now write a poem using onomatopoeic words. Your poem can be about anything you like!

## Other unusual words

Use a dictionary to see if you can find out what these unusual types of words are.

- Palindrome
- Anagram
- Semordnilap
- Isogram

# USING POETRY IN YOUR STORIES

Poems aren't the only place you can find poetry. Stories can benefit from some flashes of poetic language, too.

**Simile**

The giant peach, with the sunlight glinting on its side, was like a massive golden ball sailing upon a silver sea.

**Alliteration**

Can you use the techniques you've learned about in this book to add some poetry to your story-writing? Rewrite each sentence below using poetic language.

Jon ran very fast along the street.

Like a rocket, Jon zoomed along the road.

Sam was really lost in the forest.

_____

It was morning, and the sun was shining brightly.

_____

It began to rain softly.

_____

Amira wasn't scared. Not one bit.

_____

## Ideas box

Have you used any:

• alliteration (page 48)?

• similes (page 52)?

• metaphors (page 56)?

• kennings (page 60)?

Imagine a story where the hero opens an old book and finds a magic spell written as a poem. What could the spell do?



What kind of poem will the spell be? Circle the one you have chosen.

**a riddle**          **a limerick**          **a haiku**          **an acrostic poem**

Now write your magic spell as a poem.

What happens after your hero has read out your spell poem? Write the rest of the story using the poetic techniques you've learned about in this book.

# SPARK THE SENSES

There are five senses: sight, sound, touch, smell and taste. Writing often focuses on sight, but if you include sound, touch, smell or taste, you can make your poem come alive.

**Touch**

The wind stung Sophie's cheeks. It made her eyes water. It whipped her head back and whistled in her ears.

**Sound**

Match the descriptions to the settings.

It was a wet and slimy hiding place.

inside a giant's mouth

She was lying on skin that was soft and warm and almost velvety.

inside a snozzcumber

She caught a whiff of his evil-smelling breath. It stank of bad meat.

in the BFG's ear

Imagine you've been snatched by a giant's hairy hand.

How does it feel?

Imagine the BFG in Buckingham Palace, eating cake for the first time.

How does it taste?

Imagine standing next to nine sleeping giants.

How does it smell?

Remember to use all of the amazing words you thought of on pages 32–35!

The BFG's amazing hearing helps him to catch dreams in Dream Country, creep through London at night, and find the Queen's bedroom in Buckingham Palace.

If you had amazing hearing, where would you go? Why? Plan your idea below.

What would this place sound like? Write a description to set the scene for your poem.

Now write your poem. Remember to describe the setting using all five senses!

## Sensory scribbles

Find a favourite object in your home, and place it on a piece of paper. How can you describe the object using your senses? Write your ideas down. You could use a piece of fruit, a toy or a woolly hat. Remember – don't use your sense of taste on anything that isn't food!

# LUMINOUS LOLLIES

The things you choose to write about in your poems don't have to exist already. You can invent anything at all and name it whatever you like, just like in Roald Dahl's stories!

Willy Wonka also invented new technology, like transporting chocolate through television. Read the names of some of Willy Wonka's inventions in the ideas box. What do you think they look like? Draw some of them below.

### Ideas box

strawberry-juice
water pistols

luminous lollies

wriggle-sweets

toffee-apple trees

exploding sweets

magic hand-fudge

What new technology or machine would you design to help Willy Wonka? Draw your idea below and give it a name.

Imagine Willy Wonka has asked you to help make a new sweet. What would you call it? What does it look like? Draw your creation in the space below.

Write a description of one of the things you made up on page 77.

Choose your adjectives carefully to make the description really believable!

Write a poem about your new invention.

## Words need meaning!

Make sure you keep a record of all the words
you make up for your poems. Add a definition
for each one, so that you can remember what
your wonderful words mean.

# FAST AS A FIZZLECRUMP

Long and short sentences can change the pace of your poem.
A very long sentence can give a sense of a long time or a great
distance. Lots of short sentences can give a sense of speed.

Imagine you are on a fast train at night. Write a poem about what you see from your window,
using lots of short sentences.

"Attention, please! Attention, please!
Don't dare to talk! Don't dare to sneeze!
Don't doze or daydream! Stay awake!
Your health, your very life's at stake!
Ho-ho, you say, they can't mean me.
Ha-ha, we answer, wait and see."

> Her father came the second day
> And fetched her in a Chevrolet,
> And drove her to their home in Dover.

Write a poem about a long journey using long sentences. Use conjunctions to join ideas together and make your sentences as long as possible. Use the ideas box for some suggestions.

## Ideas box

and     or

so      when

but     because

## Speedy reading

Find a paragraph from a book you like. Read it carefully. Does it use short sentences or long ones? What kind of atmosphere is it trying to create? Try reading the passage aloud – first quickly, then slowly. Which sounded better?

Imagine being a helicopter pilot flying over your home for the first time. What would you see? How would it feel? Plan your ideas in the spaces below.

Write a poem about the helicopter pilot's journey. Use different sentence lengths to change the pace of your poem.

## Pacy poems

You could also write a poem about:

- being shrunk so you are very tiny
- exploring under the sea
- fireworks
- two snails racing in the park.

Think about how you can use sentence length to add effect to your poems!

# PHIZZWIZARD OR TROGGLEHUMPER?

Dreams are a great inspiration for poems and stories. The BFG has caught lots of different types of dreams.

Look at these four dream types. What do you think might happen in each one? Write your ideas in the jars.

**Golden Phizzwizards**
the best dreams imaginable

**Ringbellers**
silly, funny dreams

### Winksquifflers
sweet and pleasant dreams

### Trogglehumpers
the worst – a bogrotting nightmare!

The BFG can mix different dreams together to make up new ones. Choose two dreams from pages 84 and 85, and mix them together. What could happen? Plan your new dream in the space below.

Is your new dream a ringbeller, a golden phizzwizard, a winksquiffler or a trogglehumper?

Write a poem about your dream below. Think of believable details and use descriptive language so the reader can imagine your dream.

Remember to use your five senses when you create your dream poem!

**Dream journal**

Keep a notepad and pencil by your bed so you can write down your dreams when you wake up. Use them for inspiration for your poetry!

# MY PHENOMENAL POETRY

Marvellous work – you've learned so many splendiferous new things! Use these balloons to write down your favourite new phrases and words. When you write your next poem, you can look at these balloons to help you remember them.

Scintillating similes

like    as

Shut out all normal surroundings and go flying away to a magic world where everything is enchanting and fantastic.

Magnificent metaphors

# Amazing alliteration

assonance

alliteration

# Carefully crafted kennings

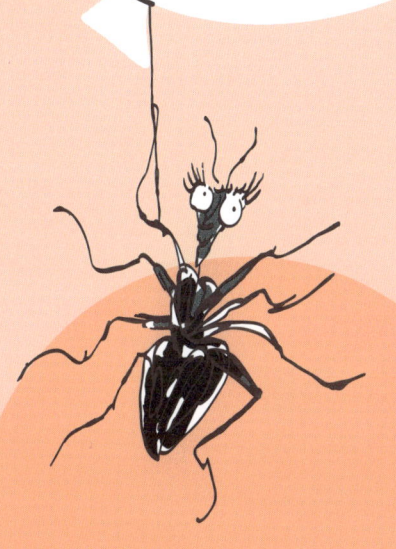

# YOU ARE A WRITER!

Poetry is a wonderful way to share your thoughts and ideas. It can also help you to think more carefully about the words you use when writing stories.

An anthology is a collection of different poems. Use these next few pages to write lots of different types of poems for an anthology of your own. They can be about anything you like! Use the tips on pages 6 and 7 for extra help.

## My first anthology

Once you have written your poems out, you could copy them on to pieces of paper, then tie them together with ribbon or string to make your very first book of poetry! Use coloured paper, draw your own illustrations, come up with a title for your collection, and make it look lovely!